Four Arrows In My Hand

Parenting Principles for Aiming Your Greatest Weapon

By Terrilyn Franklin

Dedication

This book is dedicated to my mother, Juanita Hood, affectionately known as Mama Hood. She was my biggest cheerleader. She showed me how a wise woman builds. She loved her family (and others) so well.

Foreword

I count it a special privilege and honor to write a foreword for *Four Arrows in My Hand.*

This book is a "how to" testimonial and manual filled with practical examples, advice and godly pearls about how, based on the Word of God and dependence on the Holy Spirit, we as parents can successfully raise up godly children that can go out and engage in life battles and win.

I have known and observed Pastor Terrilyn and her family closely for many years and I can truly state that this book is a testimonial of her life. She and her husband have successfully raised four powerful arrows by yielding to the Spirit and the word of God

As I read through this fascinating book in one sitting I could not but think on this scripture passage:

"Wisdom is justified by her children .... wisdom is shown to be right by the lives of those who follow it." (Luke 7;35)

This book is a must read for any biological, surrogate, or spiritual parent seeking practical guidelines on how to raise up strong confident well-balanced godly children in this generation.

I strongly recommend it without reservations.

Mope Akintorin MD
Pediatrician and mother

Contents

Introduction

It seems like God always inspires my writings while I am in His presence. While worshipping and jumping at a Fire Conference I heard the Lord say *Four Arrows in My Hand*. I want you to write about the arrows I have placed in your quiver. I want you to share the principles I taught you about raising four daughters, prophetesses and worshippers for my Kingdom. Hear my heart about how God led me on my journey.

I have always loved the idea of family. I come from a pretty big one, and I can remember as a little girl thinking one day I would get married and have my very own. My mother is one of twelve children. She grew up in the south, in Natchez, Mississippi. She was the most incredible mother, and she loved her family. We had the house that was a safe place for all. I can remember young adults coming into our home and feeling welcomed because my mother had a heart for young people. They affectionately called my mom "Mama Hood!" When children did not know how to talk to their parents, my mother was a safe place. She was that older wise mother. She never tore down anyone's parenting style, and she always tried to help the children heal or reconcile with their parents.

Our girls have a rich spiritual legacy on their father's side as well. My husband comes from a godly family. His parents were founders and pastors of the church where he was raised. He and his siblings served as the musicians and ministry leaders. His parents have twelve children and all of them are still serving the Lord to this day. This could probably be attributed to the fact that his mom still prays daily for each of her children, their spouses, and her grandchildren — and this is easily well over fifty people. When my husband was younger, he remembers his father raising a newborn baby girl from the dead (that is another discussion). This heritage belongs to our seed.

Every family has a heritage that is passed down to their children. The question is, what is your heritage and what will your heritage be?

Heritage can refer to practices or characteristics that are passed down through the years, from one generation to the next. Researching your family tree would help you gain a sense of your personal heritage. Heritage is often used to discuss a cultural aspect or tradition that has been passed down through generations.

Your heritage can be positive or negative. In my research I found that my family had a strong heritage of prayer and supernatural gifts. When my mother was a child, she told us how her family would get up around 4am to go to the deep woods of Woodville, MS, to her grandparents' house. Her grandparents, the grandchildren and their parents would come together, and they would pray for the family and whatever needs the Lord assigned them to cover in prayer. I can even remember growing up and having prayer meetings at our home. This was a family heritage that I grabbed, and I passed down to my children. It is not enough for us to have a spiritual inheritance and our children never experience it.

ARROWS

"Train the child in the way he should go and when he is
old he will not depart".
(Proverbs 22:6)

T *he way he should go?* The *way* is the target. The target
he should hit. Aim him in the direction of the path
that leads to his target.

"4 As arrows are in the hand of a mighty man;
so are children of the youth. 5 Happy is the man
that hath his quiver full of them: they shall not be
ashamed, but they shall speak with the
enemies in the gate."
(Psalm 127:4-5)

Like arrows in the hand of a warrior, so are children.
We are aiming arrows at a target. This ties into looking

on the ways of the child because HE has a way that he should go.

Awaken warrior out of a deep sleep. Recognize your mission, if you should agree to accept (even if you don't agree), is to look at your children differently and see your role differently. A warrior is strong and mighty according to Strong's Concordance. Parents, God does not see our position as passive, weak or fearful. We are champions, fighters, heroes, soldiers, battlers, combatants, conscripts, troopers enlisted, servicemen. Our children are our greatest weapon, our arrows. A warrior uses his arrows to accomplish his warfare. Our children have kingdom assignments that we aim them towards every day.

Also, the scripture mentions "in the hand". Hand is singular, and some people would see this as a weakness because the scripture only mentions one hand. Many parents may feel alone whether they are single or married. Hand is singular. I want you to know it is not about the number of hands on the arrow - it is about the hand representing authority. This is the time to ask the Lord for His plan for your arrow and begin to aim.

Train up a child in the way he should go and when he is old, he shall not depart. Each child has a bent or course for his life. We sometimes have a tendency to use knowledge gained through an encounter with one individual child's pattern or we may adopt our parents' methods used to raise us, and we make our experience a blanket truth for every child we have stewardship over. But we must remember each child is unique and we have to be sensitive to the time that we live in and constantly stay alert to changes around both our children and us. We cannot assume anything because once you think you've found something that works, they switch on you. My hat is off to those parents who are able to multitask and have managed to produce some unique children even though society says the odds are against them.

In days past mothers were more aware because mothers spent more time in the home. Nowadays parents spend more time out of the home than in the home. I received an email about "Old School Mothers" and how they did not allow their children to be idle nor did they miss an opportunity to deal with character issues in their children.

In the 21st century most parents don't challenge their children in the area of character and don't seem to realize its importance in their child's development. We push education, we push religion, and we push extra-curricular activities; however, when it comes to character issues we laugh at our children's behavior, or we feel sorry that people don't understand our children and are mistreating them. We may even have some of the same issues, so we feel that it is normal to act in that way. A child is known by his ways, and a child left to himself will bring his mother to shame.

"The character of even a child is known by how he acts, by whether his deeds are pure and right." (Proverbs 20:11)

"The rod and reproof give wisdom: but a child left to himself bringeth his mother to shame." (Proverbs 29:15)

Childhood is when character is developed. When we do our part, we save our children from having God develop their character when they are grown.

When the family was created it was always with generations in mind. For instance, whenever God was mentioned it was said of Him to be "the God of Abraham, Isaac and Jacob". Our families should always think about the next generation.

"5 And Joshua said unto them, Pass over before the ark of the Lord your God into the midst of Jordan, and take you up every man of you a stone upon his shoulder, according unto the number of the tribes of the children of Israel: 6 That this may be a sign among you, that when your children ask their fathers in time to come, saying, What mean ye by these stones? 7 Then ye shall answer them, That the waters of Jordan were cut off before the ark of the covenant of the Lord; when it passed over Jordan, the waters of Jordan were cut off: and these stones shall be for a memorial unto the children of Israel forever."

(Joshua 4:5-7)

The scripture told the children of Israel to build memorials so that as their children would walk by with them and observe the memorials, they would ask about them. Then they could use memorials as teaching moments. Our children should be walking with us during their growth and development stages (not on their own, yet).

FAMILY

"1 One day, the Eternal One called out to Abram.
Eternal One: Abram, get up and go! Leave your
country. Leave your relatives and your father's
home, and travel to the land I will show you. Don't
worry—I will guide you there. 2 I have plans to
make a great people from your descendants. And I
am going to put a special blessing on you and cause
your reputation to grow so that you will become a
blessing and example to others."
(Genesis 12:1-2)

I find it very interesting that God tells Abraham to leave
his family. Why? I want to make of you a great nation.
Okay, but family is where everything begins. Even growing up in a Godly family, you still need to follow God's

plans for your family. I believe in honoring the generations before. It is a kingdom principle, but why did God call Abraham to leave his family? God wanted Abraham to leave his family's ideologies that are contrary to God's plan and vision for the family. In Abraham's case God was leading him to another land. In our case God may not be asking you to leave physically, but we have to leave spiritually and sometimes emotionally. We have to resist the tendencies of our family dictating what is appropriate behavior for our children, prescribing their opinion on how you should govern your family and your family's God-given assignment. You have to avoid the "isms and schisms" that pervert the plan of God for your offspring. You can't have any double mindedness. God had to get Abraham alone, away from his family's mindset. It has been said that Abraham's family worshipped idols. Abraham needed to learn what God's voice sounded like. Do you know what God's voice sounds like versus the status quo? Is His voice distinguishable? We need to hear without distractions. During this time there was no bible. There were no scriptures that every family owned in their homes. Today we can read the bible to learn how God wants our families to live, but Abraham was pioneering what his covenant promise would look like as our example. This was truly a walk by faith because he had no other pattern to follow.

God has always had a plan for the family, but the enemy also has a plan for our families. When God first established the family in Genesis, it was very clear that God wanted the family to be a mirror of heaven. Yes! Man fell in the Garden of Eden through Eve, who was deceived by the serpent. Then she invited her husband to eat the forbidden fruit with her, which created a spiral effect that caused the world to die spiritually. This spiritual disconnection affected man's relationship with God. This also brought chaos into the world because man lost his place of dominion in the earth. Now our Kingdom assignment is for the families of the earth to return to God and return to our dominion.

COMMAND

"17 And the LORD said, Shall I hide from Abraham that thing which I do; 18 Seeing that Abraham shall surely become a great and mighty nation, and all the nations of the earth shall be blessed in him? 19 For I know him, that he will command his children and his household after him, and they shall keep the way of the LORD, to do justice and judgment; that the LORD may bring upon Abraham that which he hath spoken of him."
(Genesis 18:17-19)

Some people find it harsh to think that we should command our children after God. As a matter of fact, I have heard parents get defensive about commanding their children after God. "Children should make their own choice when it comes to choosing faith," is what some parents say. "We do not want to force them."

We command our children to brush their teeth. We command our children to wash their faces. We command our children to clean their rooms. We command them to go to sleep at a decent hour to prepare for school the next day. We command our children to do their homework. We command our children to get good grades. We command our children to get an education. We command our children to play sports or a musical instrument. We command our children by taking them to practice for sport teams, so that they can have discipline, maybe even get a scholarship. We command our children to go to college to get a degree. But when it comes to THE MOST IMPORTANT subject, God, we let them choose. Some feel that "command" seems too strong of a word when it comes to the things of God. However, it is the word that God uses to describe the assignment of the Father of Nations.

BENEFITS

"3 And God Almighty bless thee, and make thee fruitful, and multiply thee, that thou mayest be a multitude of people; 4 And give thee the blessing of Abraham, to thee, and to thy seed with thee; that thou mayest inherit the land wherein thou art a stranger, which God gave unto Abraham."
(Genesis 28:3-4)

The promise in Genesis 28:3-4 was given to Abraham, the father of nations. This is the blessing that God gave to solidify a Godly heritage. This was the command God gave to ensure that every promise made to Abraham would be fulfilled. This is the command that God gave so that all the families of the earth (cultures & ethnicities) would be blessed. Fathers and mothers are responsible for generational blessings being passed down to their children.

"Generational Blessings" is a benefit of commanding your children after GOD! This is why we see in scripture that this promise is to Abraham, Isaac, and Jacob. This is generational!! Abraham (Grandparent), Isaac (Father), and Jacob (Child) were given this blessing. I love this! The concept that blessings can be passed down in your bloodline is very clear, all the way down to your grandchildren. I have learned as a parent that kids don't automatically know what to do or when to do it. As parents we have to develop by moving from nurturer to commander.

God wants our children blessed more than we do. He wants to spare them from the consequences of wrong decisions, bad influences, guilt and shame. We can help them in this process by keeping God's plan for the family at the forefront of our parenting.

We must let go of adopting the world's perspective and get back on our faces before the Lord to receive a kingdom perspective. We must make a declaration to the enemy, "Not my daughter, not my son. I am not releasing them to you. I will not give up my authority and cry in hopelessness or despair." God has a plan for your children. Begin to ask God why He allowed your womb to be open, why He placed children in your care, or why He put you in an influential position, enabling you to pour into other parents. We are all on assignment and the goal is to return back to God's intention. Let's learn how to begin to partner with the Lord and see God's purposes unfold in the life of our inheritance.

PRINCIPLE #5

CULTURE

The western culture does not truly understand the term "mother" or "parent." Mother/Parent is not placed in the house to spoil the children, nor placed in the family to badger the children. Neither are we there to coddle their behavior. We are there to nurture and sharpen the gifts that God has placed in our home.

While holding your precious baby in your arms, society is waiting with a path already mapped out for their life. They tell you by age three, send them to pre-school to give them an educational advantage. If they miss pre-school, no need to worry, just send them to kindergarten so they can begin their primary education. Wait, don't stop there. Let us have them at age 18 (because they are legally grown). Now they are ready to go away to college.

You may be reading this thinking, *Yes that is the goal,* because we think this is the norm. However, should we give our children's education over to the culture of the day? We should have a greater influence in our children's lives. Children gain opportunities that they may have missed when parents are involved in their education. This is true *first* in the natural and *then* in the spiritual. People always think the opposite. Let's learn how to begin to partner with the Lord and see God's purposes unfold in the life of God's inheritance.

Many parents are sending their children away from their homes unprepared. For starters, parents are depending upon an ungodly society to educate children properly. Parents have gotten so far from God's original plan, which is found in the teaching of scripture.

"5 You shall love the LORD your God with all your heart and with all your soul and with all your might. 6 These words, which I am commanding you today, shall be on your heart. 7 You shall teach them diligently to your sons and shall talk of them when you sit in your house and when you walk by the way and when you lie down and when you rise up".
(Deuteronomy 6:5-7)

The Old Testament passage in Deuteronomy, commands parents to teach their children. Instead we have our children learn at the hands of others without any input from us. Parents were commanded to teach their children. Children were never expected to find their way.

Dating

The American meaning of dating is unhealthy. It evokes emotional and physical ramifications that can have detrimental lifetime effects.

I am raising four daughters. As I have watched the dating scene, I have concluded my daughters will not date. As you look at the history of dating you find a lot of flaws in this model. In my research of other cultures, I have found dating is a part of the American culture, however it is a deadly poison that is proven to have emotional & physical ramifications with detrimental lifetime effects.

Why Emotions?

Emotions are the first thing that happen in dating. People begin to get attached because of emotions they feel at the moment. When time is spent alone developing these feelings, they become connected on an emotional level.

Emotions create a response in the mind that arises spontaneously, rather than through conscious effort. Emotions can be undesired to the individual feeling them; he or she may wish to control them but often cannot. Thus, one of the most distinctive, and perhaps challenging facts about human nature, is this potential for entanglement, or even opposition, between will, emotion, and reason (Wikipedia). As a result, they want to spend more time together, desiring to make the other person happy, because they feel that will make them happy. At this level they don't really know the other person's character or personality because they are so busy trying to impress each other. These emotions can lead into a new direction, which can become physical.

Why Physical?

Getting physical becomes the next step because when people are involved emotionally, they often get into trouble. When you have people in a confined place with emotions that are running wild you tend to get into more physical expressions. This may start with kissing. The next step is petting. Then the next step is heavy petting. Because these choices normally happen when you are alone with no supervision and no restraints and some people cannot handle the pressure. Also, we know that physical contact can lead to teen pregnancy and other emotional decisions or mistakes.

Additionally, about one in three high school students have been or will be involved in an abusive relationship. Forty percent of teenage girls ages 14 to 17 say they know someone their age who has been hit or beaten by a boyfriend. Teen dating violence most often takes place in the home of one of the partners. In 1995, 7 percent of all murder victims were young women who were killed by their boyfriends. One in five or 20 percent of dating couples report some type of violence in their relationship. One of five college females will experience some form of dating violence. A survey of 500 young women, ages 15 to 24, found that 60 percent were currently involved in an ongoing abusive relationship and all participants had experienced violence in a dating relationship. One study found that 38 percent of date rape victims were young women from 14 to 17 years of age. A survey of adolescent and college students revealed that date rape accounted for 67 percent of sexual assaults. More than half of young women raped (68 percent) knew their rapist either as a boyfriend, friend or casual acquaintance. Six out of 10 rapes of young women occur in their own home or a friend or relative's home, not in a dark alley. More than four in every 10 incidents of domestic violence involve non-married persons. (Bureau of Justice Special Report: Intimate Partner Violence, May 2001) (Other statistic from the U.S. Department of Justice) (Dating Violence, (ACADV)- http://www.acadv.org/dating.html)

By now I guess you're wondering what a safe alternative is. Courtship is a proven model that has been used for centuries. Courtship is the idea of getting to know someone for the PURPOSE of marriage. The difference in courting and dating is the person would court to marry as opposed to dating, which is to be with another person socially on a regular basis: go out, causing an emotional tie. Courtship always starts in a setting with a group of people having fun. The group could go to a game or out to eat. There is accountability in a group setting. The more time you spend in a group setting the more you develop a relationship that is built on friendship. Friends enjoy each other's company. Friends are invited to be a part of family functions. This creates a safe environment where they don't have to pretend because there is nothing but being themselves. It is also a model that many countries still continue. In Amish culture courtship is the model in use and their divorce rate is 1/2% (I believe divorce is linked to dating). Filipinos and Native American use courtship as their models. Emotional level is last in their process. When an individual is ready to be with a person it is in this safe place that this individual recognizes if someone is worthy of his or her emotions. The interested party would have observed this person in a group setting. After this time, the interested party can decide if he wants to pursue this person for marriage. Then seek counsel from trusted individuals such as their parents or people they respect and trust.

In conclusion, when my daughters pursue the model of courtship, they limit the possibility of regrets, shame, a broken heart, emotional scars, depression, or unnecessary baggage. You often have one or all of those with dating. They won't have anyone to compare their spouse to when it is time for marriage. You will if you dated and took it to a physical level with or without your consent. (I also believe suicide numbers would decrease as well as murders by "ex-boyfriends or girlfriends.) When it is time to get married, they will be more willing to endure because they have not practiced divorce, which is similar to breaking up in dating. Therefore, they will be healthy and whole with no detrimental effects that will follow them throughout their lives opposed to dating.

Voices

When one of my daughters was in high school, she was on the phone with a male friend at 11pm at night. I mentioned to her that it was getting late. I was teaching her, while young and speaking with a young man who was not very respectful of how she was being raised, that ladies should not be on the phone late at night. When she shared this with him that it was getting late and ladies should not be on the phone all time of night, he proceeded to tell her that she is still a beautiful young lady (and that) he does not look at her differently. He did not agree with that reason to get off the phone. She obeyed me anyway; however, she began to share this young man's opinion with me. I have never had a problem with any of my children having male friends. However, I did raise them in a way that was pretty foreign to today's parenting. This young man had already made fun of how she was being raised, yet they were still friends. But I was aware. After she shared with confidence the young man's opinion of her, I asked her to give me her cell phone. She had a very bizarre look on her face. I proceeded to inform her that until my voice is louder than any other voice, she will not have a cell phone. Later that night while I had the phone the young man texted her apologizing. Telling her how beautiful she is, and she should obey her parents. He expressed that the way she is being raised is what makes her so attractive. He exclaimed, "This is why I know you are my wife and we will get married." This text came at 2am on a school night. This young man was not aware that I was receiving the message. This text could have brought so much struggle and confusion for my daughter. Creating more opportunity to hear his voice over mine. She did not get the phone until my voice was louder than any other voice.

PRINCIPLE #6

DISCERN

As parents, have we taught our children to discern their environments? Discernment would enable them to recognize a possible Virginia Tech situation or Northern Illinois University massacre. As a result of their discernment, have we taught them to speak up about injustices within their schools? Do they recognize or know how to respond if they feel that a teacher is mishandling their authority? By default, MTV, the internet, television, Children Ministry, and public/private schools are educating our children. By default, parents are no longer the primary educator; they are giving up their responsibility. Children still need their parents' support and guidance.

It is amazing when you look at Isaac when Abraham took him to the mountain to worship. The young lad was submitted to his father. It has been said that he was between the age of seventeen and twenty years old. In the scriptures he was considered a lad. He trusted his father's leadership and knew he feared the Lord. He had been taught about sacrifice because Isaac said to his father that he saw the wood for the sacrifice, but then asked where the sacrifice was. Another teaching moment from his father was that the Lord HIMSELF would provide a sacrifice.

> "Abraham said to his young men, 'Stay here with
> the donkey, and I and the lad will go over there;
> and we will worship and return to you.'"
> (Genesis 22:5)

In this day and age, we would call him a man. Many parents have begun to accept the mindset that at 18 our children are grown. Many children are turned over to their own devices when they still need some instruction as they navigate this milestone. This is why many have difficult times in college. They have not been given the proper supervision or encouragement through difficult adulting moments. No one was there to provide wisdom and intervention when they needed intervention. Education is important, but parents should be their children's advocate and steward as long as they still need wisdom and direction.

We are entrusting our children to the educational system. Parents no longer know how their children are doing in school until grades come out. Parents are no longer aware that their children are in academic trouble because they are not involved in the process. Parents no longer know the names of their children's teachers. They have delegated their responsibility to the education system, trusting the system to be flawless and the environment to be safe. In the end their children have been susceptible to detrimental effects that parents usually find out about when it is too late.

EDUCATION

In one of my daughters' eighth grade year, I decided to put her in a private school. The private school requested a copy of her permanent record. In case you did not know, a permanent record contains academic grades throughout grammar school. I realized that two of her grades were incorrect in two main subjects. The grades were "C's" that should have been "A's." Although I proved this was incorrect, I was told to handwrite the corrections in pencil and give it to the new school. Now if I had written in the grades the record would not be considered permanent. So after my persistence the permanent record was updated.

Three years later I requested a copy of another daughter's permanent record. It happened again in the same household at the same school – I was given an inaccurate report. Can you believe it? My second daughter's grades were incorrect. She had been given the wrong grades for sixth grade (she was now in eighth grade). Also, none of her honor courses or foreign language grades were documented. What if I had left the educational process solely up to the system? What if I were not involved and had no communication with the school? This could have marred her chances of receiving a high school scholarship for college. This is why we parents have to be involved in the educational process. We can't let the educational system have our children without any parental partnership in their education. It took the school three months to update those records, with my constant follow-up.

I had another daughter who had received a "D" on her report card that did not make sense. According to her grades she should have received a "B." Over the course of several meetings with the teacher, then the assistant principal, and later the principal, we figured out the problem. The teacher had put the wrong weights in the computer for the grade averages. Can you believe it? The teacher was depending on technology to get the grade right. All of the students' grades were calculated wrong. The computer calculations were improperly calculated. Just out of curiosity I asked, "What would have happened had I not been involved?" The teacher stated, "We probably would have found it out about three to four months later, but we would have found it." Our children's education has to be more important than trusting a flawed system to work without parental partnership. God intended parents to be involved.

I have a friend whose daughter had just made sixteen and received her associate degree. Even though she was in college her mother was very much involved. You may be thinking, well she is only sixteen and in college - her mother should be involved. This young lady took a lot of free courses. However, if her mom had not been involved, she would not have known all the free classes that were available to her before she went to college. She would not have the full scholarship that she received. My friend and her daughter stayed in close contact with the guidance counselor, all in an effort to ensure that her daughter was meeting the required standards for graduation. After two years she had what was needed to graduate per her counselor. While preparing the documentations for graduation she was hit with a requirement that the counselor had not communicated. Although the parent was involved the school still made a mistake. However, the parent was able to mediate the outcome. In the end the counselor was dealt with for providing erroneous information. This brings me back to my point. What if there had been no parental involvement in this process?

Parents we cannot afford the cost of being absent. Our children are experiencing unnecessary frustration. Thousands of dollars continue to be spent to correct mistakes because of a lack of involvement in our children's lives. What about a deficiency in biblical understanding that would have prepared them for life? The book of Proverbs offers the best lessons on life. Most of these mistakes are occurring because many have stopped functioning in our God-given roles as the primary educator of our children. There is nothing wrong with utilizing the systems that are in place, but we cannot rely on them or neglect our parental responsibility to train them in the way they should go. We must be involved in the educational process. We are not done until they are married and no longer our responsibility, but even then, our role changes to counselor and not commander.

DISCERNMENT VERSUS JUDGEMENT

The ability to discern is in all mothers, and I am certain those who have not given birth also have this ability. The world calls it "intuitiveness" or "that inner voice." But God calls it "discernment." Some need it developed more than others. Many of us need to spend more time developing this ability. Parenting has been evolving more into self-centeredness. We are so consumed with the details of the household, work and ministry that we overlook the children. We are just too busy to look and listen. Children are always speaking, verbally and non-verbally. We are taught that communication is 20% verbal and 80% nonverbal.

Our culture has so many voices that say: Let your children do their own thing, let them date early, and let them make their own decisions. In the meantime, while our children are making their own decisions, parents have a tendency to go into the closet and say, "Oh Lord, I hope they make the right choices." Instead, we should stay involved and foster a relationship where there are no secrets, but open communication, even if it is hard for us to sit and hear what they need to share.

Parents should not walk around in fear like a Dr. Sleuth, but we should always be aware of those times when we sense, "I need to linger a little longer;" "I need to check up and see who she is talking to;" or "I need to find out why my child seems a little withdrawn today." Parents and caregivers need to listen for a change in their child's conversation. Has your child picked up some new phrases or has your child begun to speak rudely or impolitely? Take a look at your child's phone, computer, or tablet's history. Why?

My intention in this book is not to make any parent feel guilty for any missed opportunities or to make any child feel anger or unforgiveness toward any parent for missing a season in his or her life. I pray that it will bring enlightenment. When read with an open heart, this book can cause relationships to be healed and its revelations can cause the hearts of parents to turn to their children and the hearts of children to turn to their parents.

Discern the Season

"54 And he said also to the people, When ye see a cloud rise out of the west, straightway ye say, There cometh a shower; and so it is. 55 And when ye see the south wind blow, ye say, There will be heat; and it cometh to pass. 56 Ye hypocrites, ye can discern the face of the sky and of the earth; but how is it that ye do not discern this time? 57 Yea, and why even of yourselves judge ye not what is right?"
(Luke 12:54-57)

We can tell by the signs in the sky whether there will be rain or if the sun will shine. Similarly, we gain knowledge of the systems of this world by the way the political system functions and stock market trends. We observe certain symptoms in our bodies and know what medicine to take. We can tell how our body functions under stress. We can tell when others are angry with us or happy with us by their behavior. We have been to some of the best schools in the world (and even the school of hard knocks).

We are reading all kinds of fiction novels and we can learn how to build new relationships. But if you ask the church how the kingdom of God functions, in regard to our family or children, we communicate knowledge gained from this world's system. We do not give a synopsis based on the principles of God's kingdom. Jesus told the Pharisees you have all this knowledge yet you cannot discern the times (season). Parents we have not been prepared to discern the season of our children.

Discern

The basic meaning of the term *discern* is a "physical apprehension", whether through sight, touch, or hearing. Darkness sometimes makes "recognition" impossible. (Ruth 3:14) People are often "recognized" by their voices. (Judges 18:3) Nakar sometimes means "pay attention to," a special kind of "recognition": "Blessed be the man who took notice of you" (Ruth 2:19), "did take knowledge of". This verb can mean "to be acquainted with," a kind of intellectual awareness: "…neither shall his place know him any more". (Job 7:10)

The sense of "to distinguish" is seen in the scripture, "...the people could not discern the noise of the shout of joy from the noise of the weeping of the people..." (Ezra 3:13)

(From Vine's Expository Dictionary of Biblical Words, Copyright (c)1985, Thomas Nelson Publishers)

Basically, the more time you spend in any specific area or with any specific person the more you begin to develop an ability to discern that person or the situation.

Seasons

Children are constantly changing and the more outside influences they encounter the greater the potential is for the wrong influences to penetrate. Therefore, we need to understand seasons.

As I prepared to write this PRINCIPLES on seasons, I had the wrong perspective. I was trying to describe each season based on the world's perspective. Often, seasonal changes bring on complaints and grumbling from those who don't want the current season to end, instead of appreciation for each season for the purposes God has intended. I.e., spring is often cold and windy and the time for planting and bringing forth new life; summer is hot and represents the time for growing and maturing; fall is a rather pleasant time of year and purposed for gathering the harvest; and the winter season is cold and bitter, but it kills the germs in the earth and prepares the earth to begin a new cycle of life.

The Christian family has accepted this perspective of living for seasons we consider pleasant and begrudging the discomfort of adverse weather conditions with no thought of God's purposes for each season or appreciating what is gained from each. This perspective has caused us to go through some seasons a lot longer than God intended, while we come to the understanding of what God is trying to show us. We first have to stop complaining about the change before we submit and make the necessary adjustments in our minds. As I began to meditate, I then received God's perspective. When I think of spring, I think of seeds being planted, flowers budding and trees beginning to bud with the potential of green leaves.

When I think of summer I think of green grass, the beautiful fruit trees, some in full bloom, and beautiful summer days and nights. I think of family picnics, sweet watermelon, beaches and swimming. My husband, who is an artist, loves autumn because of the beauty that comes as the leaves turn to vibrant colors. Then there is the winter, which puts me in the mind of beautiful snowflakes, a time of snowball fights, sledding, ice skating and so on. I especially think of a Thomas Kinkade picture of a cottage at the end of a snow-covered driveway whose roof is covered with snow. Just the scene makes me want to cozy up and enjoy family. Here is the perspective that God has intended for our families to understand.

There is beauty in every season; however, each season requires different types of preparation and maintenance as we enter into it to abide for the time necessary to accomplish God's purposes. This is how it is in the lives of our family members; we just have to spend time preparing and maintaining. Each season reflects its individual beauty in our lives and in the lives of our children.

Discernment Developed

Discernment can be developed when more and more time is spent with a child. Parents have been spending less

time than ever with their children and we are responding to behavior rather than discerning our children. We
need to get to the root of our children's behavior. Not the
symptoms. The more we learn our children's character the
more we can discern and the more effective we become
as parents, guardians or stewards over God's inheritance.

The ultimate discernment is when you spend time in
God's Word learning to discern the devil's influence in
creating problems. Then we can be more effective in con-
fronting Satan's lies. If we are immature in the Word of
God, instead of bringing a child into the plans that God
has for him we will begin to judge the child and bring
condemnation. We may then identify the individual as
the enemy and not recognize the negative influence that
is at work in order to develop a plan on how to be effective in our parenting.

You have to spend time in order to discern. If you
cannot discern your children then you need to ask yourself, have I invested the time? I know we are busier than
our parents were. However, our children are exposed to
far more than we were as well. There are many points
to this message. When we have invested the time, we
don't have to worry if our child does encounter a negative

influence because it does not change what is under the surface. We must continue with our preservation. What are we preserving?

Notice the following scripture and its word for *discern*.

"And he discerned him not, because his hands were
hairy, as his brother Esau's hands: so he
blessed him."
(Genesis 27:23)

In the old testament the Hebrew word for *discern* here is *nakar* (naw-kar'); (OT:5234) "a primitive root"; "properly", "to scrutinize," i.e. "look intently at"; hence (with recognition implied), "to acknowledge", "be acquainted with", "care for", "respect", "revere", or (with suspicion implied), "to disregard", "ignore", "be strange toward", "reject", "resign", "dissimulate" (as if ignorant or disowning):

NT:1253 - diakrisis (dee-ak'-ree-sis); from NT:1252; judicial estimation: KJV - discern (-ing), disputation.

The history of this word displays the same process. It says to *discern* means "to dispute" or "argue". And that leads to separating the evidence and separating the facts leading to the "final judgment".

Judgment

Strong's Exhaustive Concordance Numbers to the Greek words:

> "1 Judge not, that you be not judged. 2 For with what judgment you judge, you will be judged; and with the measure you use, it will be measured back to you."
>
> (Matthew 7:1-2)

Judge NT:2919 - krino (kree'-no); properly, to distinguish, i.e. decide (mentally or judicially); by implication, to try, condemn, punish.

In KJV it means - avenge, conclude, condemn, damn, decree, determine, esteem, judge, go to (sue at the) law, ordain, call in question, sentence, to think.

Judgment NT:2917- krima (kree'-mah); from NT:2919; a decision (the function or the effect, for or against ["crime"]): In the KJV it means - avenge, condemned, condemnation, damnation, go to law, judgment.

Judging is definitely not what we want to do because we never want our children to feel hopeless or condemned.

"But strong meat belongeth to them that are of
full age, even those who by reason of use have their
senses exercised to discern both good and evil."
(Hebrews 5:14)

The church defines *discerning* as "the gift of discerning
of spirits"; however, discernment is mentioned throughout the bible, not only as a spiritual gift.

PERSPECTIVE

Overall, some of us are parenting from a limited perspective because there is no manual that teaches us how to parent. If there was it would not apply to every child because all children are different. Some of us are parenting from our own family dysfunction or even are own fear(s). Our parents did the best they could. We all come from different backgrounds and we all have different paths to follow.

There are no cookie cutter patterns. However, we can all develop a God-given insight that will cause us to always be sensitive to the moments that we need to pause and follow through on our discerning. Mothers, we need to always be alert because there are always moments that we can miss opportunities because we

44

are continuously learning and evolving ourselves. We are not the same people we were in many ways. Since becoming parents our needs have changed too. Some have two, three, even four or more children. Help, Lord! We have to always shift gears, especially if their ages are different. We also have to be careful that we do not hold one sibling hostage because of another sibling's or another child's past challenges. Each child is an individual and we need to enter each experience with a fresh new perspective.

KEEP LOOKING

"She watches over the ways of her household, And
does not eat the bread of idleness."
(Proverbs 31:27)

I believe nothing slips up on a mother. Mothers can often ignore the signs that are presented everyday through their children. When the Word of God states that the virtuous woman looks on the ways of her family, "the ways" represents more than their physical needs. First, she looks. In order to look you have to be intentional. You can't be passive. We are not just checking in, AFTER we finish looking at all of life's distractions. By then we are exhausted.

What are we looking at when we look at our children's ways? We are seeing deeper than the surface. We see what they are doing, and we listen to what they are saying. We are observing their actions and reactions. For example, incest does not just happen. This relationship goes beyond familiarity to a point that we should investigate signs of behavioral changes or withdrawal. We are not asking questions. Rebellion does not magically appear, but develops over time, after ignoring the little signs that surface in our children. We have to be consistent in dealing with defiant behavior. Being defiant is not cute because it leads to the ugly fruit of rebellion. These situations can happen when we stop LOOKING on the WAYS of our family.

Parents, we have to get our strength back. We have to get our energy back. We have to get our focus back. I know there are more distractions now than when our parents raised us. I can remember my parents only had a television and a landline phone in our home. However, today's generation of parents are dealing with so many more distractions that are creating a divide between how the world views parenting and the original plan for our family. We live in a technological world. We have computers, the worldwide web, cell phones, iPads, tablets, Alexa and on and on. When I was growing up, it was odd for both parents to work outside of the home if you had a two-parent home. Nowadays parents are so busy and distracted that they have stopped "looking at the ways" of their home because they are barely at home. Many of us have checked out mentally, physically or emotionally. Some parents are looking for more because they have joined the "Do Me" club.

My assignment is to awaken the discerning mother or caregiver that God has placed in all of us.

I once encountered a child I knew who was playing ball outside with his friends. A boy who was older had on a new pair of shoes. The child suddenly ran home and ran into me on his way. After I greeted him, I noticed there was an unusual smirk on his face, which prompted me to ask what was going on. He told me that the older boy had new gym shoes and he felt the boy thought "he had it going on." So he went home to put on his Air Jordan's to prove that the boy did not have the "tightest" shoes. Why was that important to him? Could that be a character trait to focus on?

Once I picked up one of my daughters from school. When I touched her hand and looked at her, I sensed there was something wrong. I asked her what was bothering her and she said, "Oh mom nothing's wrong. I'm okay." I gently continued to push until she finally confided that a girl in her class had touched her private area. When she questioned her classmate, the classmate denied that she had touched her inappropriately. My daughter insisted that she did, and after the girl continued to deny it, my daughter was left feeling guilty. I asked her if it felt wrong and she said, "Yes." Then I told her it was wrong because our bodies do not lie. Then the guilt was removed from my daughter and I used that incident as a teaching moment.

PRINCIPLE #11

ACCOUNTABILITY

Parents must also be willing to be transparent with their children. When you have done something wrong admit it and it will help your child to admit his or her mistakes. Our transparency will help our children not hide their flaws from us. When we don't have a good self-image ourselves it affects how we parent, so find some parents who are doing well in the area that you are struggling in and begin to inquire about their parenting skills or get into a small parenting group.

This accountability can help you to connect with other parents who can share insights that will help you. Deal with your own rejection you have experienced so that you don't inadvertently teach it or pass rejection down to your children through your behavior. People who feel rejected often will reject others or put more expectation on the next person to perform.

When I was younger, I always knew I would have children. I never pondered it. I just determined I would have twelve. As I matured, I realized twelve was a bit much, but four would do fine. Some of my friends and even my sister was all mesmerized by babies. I thought they were cute and adorable; however, that was the extent of my fantasy. Most importantly I always wanted children that would love God and be used by Him.

Four opportunities to teach:

When You Rise Up -
In the morning

As You Walk -
As you travel to and from

As You Sit -
At mealtime or as you wait

As You Lie -
As you lie in bed

We are to train our children at every opportunity given. Just as God chose Abraham because he would command his children after God, the children of Israel were to pass down their faith to their children, so that there would not be a generation amongst his descendants that did not know God. The only way that can happen is that we as a family own the commandments in Deuteronomy 6.

There were times that God would tell the children of Israel to erect a memorial unto God after He would provide protection or perform some miracle. As a result, when the parents were walking with their children, and their children saw it, the memorial would testify and serve as a testimony of the great things that God did for the parents and the family. We need to implement this foundational truth into our families, so that our children will know the God of their parents.

PRINCIPLE #12

LEGACY

I believe God wants our children saved and to know their inheritance early in life. The bible is very clear and speaks of God as the God of Abraham, Isaac and Jacob, we know through scriptures that God is a generational God.

Salvation is to be inherited; it is the legacy of the righteous that their seed be saved. It should be the expected end of our children (A holy seed according to I Cor 7:14) from generation to generation. Legacy is something that a person leaves behind to be remembered by.

Where does legacy begin?

It begins in your house by pouring into your children.

How can you grow in discerning your legacy?

Discernment is innate in everyone. If God has made you a steward over any child; you have the ability within you to discern that child, but only after you have spent time with him. If you don't spend the time you will begin to base your opinion on other individuals. That is not fair to the child because each child and family is unique. This means you have to enter the relationship with a fresh perspective. Discernment can be developed on different levels and can be increased with the more time you spend with a child.

How is it developed?

By surrounding yourself as a parent with godly and wise mentors.

> "4 That they may teach the young women to be
> sober, to love their husbands, to love their children,
> 5 To be discreet, chaste, keepers at home, good,
> obedient to their own husbands, that the word of
> God be not blasphemed."
> (Titus 2:4-5)

Older Women

"That they may teach the young women to be
sober, to love their husbands, to
love their children…"
(Titus 2:4)

Older women need to take up their God-given responsibility to "teach what is good" in the fear of the Lord. Have you raised many children for the Lord? Then you are obviously the real expert in child rearing, and the body of Christ needs your expertise to be transmitted to the next generation. Do you have a passion for young mothers and their children?

Know that the Lord has given you that passion. Do not wait. You can begin to share your Godly wisdom with young mothers and their babies. Just remember your Titus 2 mission, and do not be deterred from it.

This scripture also means that young women need to seek out godly, older Christian women and place themselves under their instruction. No matter how godly the opinions of non-Christians may seem, we need to base our parenting on the Word of God. No matter how good motives may be, they are operating outside the plan and pattern which God has given to the church. For your own protection and the protection of your home you must not listen to them. You must not attend their classes. You must not buy their books. You must not subscribe to their newsletters. You must not watch their videos or listen to their tapes. You place yourself outside of God's plan and you place your family in peril if you do so. Place yourself instead at the feet of older women whose foundation is the Word of God.

DISCIPLINE

Discipline is never about winning. It should not be for the purpose of a parent showing the child who's who in the family. The goal is to shepherd our Child's heart to respond to correction; to redirect behavior; to cultivate Godly character. Not to reject the child, but to pull him close, so that we can make Godly deposits into his soul.

Isaac

Generational blessing is passed down to our children. This includes heritage. When Isaac was branching out on his own. The scripture said that Isaac dug the wells of his father Abraham. This is a great example of God's intention. Children should re-dig our wells of spiritual and physical inheritance. Here we see Abraham's seed, Isaac starting his own business. There was confusion in Isaac's home. He and his wife Rebecca had favorites. Having favorites is dangerous. Yes, each child is unique, and some personalities are more untreatable than others at times, but this should never cause us to choose to bring confusion in the home. When it was time for the blessings of the first born to be declared Rebecca came up with a manipulative plan to have Isaac bless Jacob (her favorite) instead of Esau (Isaac's favorite). See it is a bad thing when parents' view of parenting is completely not in unity. It can affect our arrow's (child's) course. This is another story for another time.

> "21 But Isaac said to Jacob, Come close to me, I beg of you, that I may feel you, my son, and know whether you really are my son Esau or not. 22 So Jacob went near to Isaac, and his father felt him and said, The voice is Jacob's voice, but the hands are the hands of Esau. 23 He could not identify him, because his hands were hairy like his brother Esau's hands; so he blessed him."
> (Genesis 27:21-23)

Isaac had spent enough time with his twins to discern that what he was hearing sounded more like Jacob than Esau; however, the other things he had learned to discern took precedence over what he had identified as being contrary. So he ignored his questions and proceeded. I feel this happens with many parents. We accept because it requires more time to investigate our questions. Let's just admit it. Godly parenting requires more time. You have to stay up a little longer. Ask the right questions to draw your child out into conversations that reveal his heart.

Jacob

There was a man named Jacob who had twelve sons and a daughter named Dinah. Jacob's daughter was raped, and her brothers made a decision to kill her offender instead of letting the offender marry her (because Jacob had given the rapist his permission to marry into his family). Now this story sounds so unbelievable, right? His daughter was raped. She was dishonored. Their family was dishonored. I wonder as parents if we have ever overlooked a trauma that any of our children have endured? I need you to hear how this trauma affected Jacob's children. You do not hear how Dinah is feeling. Instead you hear that a business deal was struck. An agreement was made with Dinah's rapist's family. Her brothers do not say or do anything; however, they are very angry over their sister's defilement. A requirement of the Israelites is circumcision, so the brothers came up with a plan based on their custom requiring all of the men of the land to be circumcised in order to intermarry. While the men were in pain Jacob's sons, Simeon and Levi killed all of them.

> "And Jacob said to Simeon and Levi, Ye have troubled me to make me to stink among the inhabitants of the land, among the Canaanites and the Perizzites: and I being few in number, they shall gather themselves together against me, and slay me; and I shall be destroyed, I and my house."
> (Genesis 34:30)

The children were angry over what has been done to their sister. We must pay attention to the traumas that have affected our children. Jacob thought the marriage would be a good deal that would excuse the rape. However, I wonder if God wanted Jacob to make a covenant with the men of the land that had just disgraced his family. I believe Jacob should have sought the Lord for direction on how to handle this situation. We must pray and not react. Sometimes we are so ready to move on away from the pain caused by such a horrible situation, but we are not considering the memories of those that have to live with the constant reminder of Dinah's rape with no justice, but rather a reward, permission to marry their sister and eventually the Israelite women.

He did not suspect his sons' anger in this matter. Instead of discerning his children, Jacob chose to be more concerned about his reputation in the community and how his life would be affected.

Though he had not gotten over the embarrassment they caused him, just before his death, Jacob began to speak into his children's lives. When it came time to bless them, he still remembered how Simeon and Levi embarrassed him. But God still had a plan for Jacob's children. Sometime later, Simeon's family was absorbed into Judah's tribe, and God chose the Levites as His priesthood. I believe as parents we need to separate our anger from God's anger. God loves our seed unconditionally. Just like God loves us unconditionally. He does not give us what we deserve. Don't get me wrong, our choices and our children's choices have consequences. God has spoken that. However, in the

Lord's hands we find mercy in time of need. Parents do not allow the enemy to use you to speak a curse over your seed in your anger, disappointment, or embarrassment. Ask God how you can partner with Him in this moment. Deal with the wrong choice for sure but turn it into correction or a lesson that will bring a blessing. "You did this, but you are my seed and I am looking at my grandchildren." There were things from Jacob's life and marriages that may have been manifesting through these boys. We need to quiet our soul from our feelings and ask God how we should respond to the behavior we observe. How many times have parents responded in anger over their embarrassment and not in love? When you recognize this has been your response, stop and go back and repent or say, "I am sorry for how I responded."

Prodigal Son

In the story of the prodigal son, according to the Jewish tradition, each son in each family received an inheritance out of his father's wealth. The prodigal son decided to leave the household with the blessing or prosperity that belonged to him. The boy then goes and hooks up with the wrong group of friends and begins to live lavishly.

This could be because he wanted acceptance. This son lived wastefully (riotous living - unrestrained by morality) with no thought of tomorrow, no thought of how this would affect his future and no thought of people and his environment. He only cared about the lifestyle his substance could afford him.

This son had no restraint when it came to what was right or wrong. You can look at this story from so many angles. One is how this child's heart was not dealt with before this point. Another is the pride of the first son, and finally, the parent's role in dealing with these issues early on. However, I want to deal with the response of the father after the prodigal son leaves and then returns. The way we receive our children after they mess up is important. We can accomplish more by discerning what that child needs at that moment. Let's take a look at how we have received some of the children that have come back:

I knew you were no good.

I don't know where you came from.

You are just like your no-good father.

I knew you would hurt my heart.

You will never be anything.

That's why you are broke today.

Where are your friends now?

I told you that you would need me before I need you.

I knew that you would end up like this.

Now you want to come to me to rescue you.

We have to learn to discern what the needs are at the most vulnerable time in his or her life. Many of us have partnered with the enemy against our children unconsciously. How, you ask? We do so when we respond in judgment and condemnation instead of asking, "Lord, how am I supposed to deal with this situation, so you can get the glory out of it and my child can benefit the most?" It is not only about my reputation (as in Jacob's case) it is about my stewardship because I am just a steward over God's inheritance. I am to help him to be all that God has designed him to be.

How did the prodigal son's father deal with the child that left the family's way? This father's arms were open ready to discern the need of the child. He celebrated the fact that the devil didn't kill his seed.

Wow, how many parents are willing to adopt this principle in parenting when dealing with children who have gone astray and returned? We need to develop this kind of mindset. Began to partner with God's Word and speak life instead of death. Rejoice that the devil didn't destroy my child. I can still help to restore him back to his or her place in God. I am still able to give him more substance because God has yet increased me. I can't be angry at this time because that will only cause me to shut down and hinder my peace. I can't walk in unforgiveness because it only locks me in prison. I can choose to respond with the expectation that God can restore what I thought was dead. We can find out how God can get the glory in the midst.

As long as the father was alive, he was generating more inheritance so there was something left for the boy. A lot of times because of our anger or hurt, we give the impression that there is no blessing left to our children who are less than perfect. There was more inheritance for the prodigal son because the father was still generating wealth and the son was not disowned but was still associated with his father's name.

After Isaac blessed Jacob there was still a blessing left for Esau. There was a reversal for Jabez when he cried out to God to change the stigma associated with his name.

Soul Care

What do you believe about sex? Some Christian parents are teaching their children how to have sex before marriage. Providing their children with the condoms or birth control pills. They are taking their children to the abortion clinic to get the abortion(s). This is the easy way out because many have not taught purity and the beauty of it as well as the safety of it. What do you believe about masturbation? Some parents are teaching their sons how to satisfy their own sexual needs. This is because it is a safe alternative to having sex and getting someone pregnant. However, they do not understand this creates a problem in his sexuality. This can even make it difficult for a man to be satisfied by his wife. This also can open doors to porn. God created man in such a way that when he is satisfied during sexual intercourse that he bonds to the image he is focusing on or looking at. What do you believe about R-Rated movies? Parents are allowing premature exposure to all kinds of restricted programming, completely disregarding age appropriate behavior and avoiding conversations about how a young person keeps himself pure, thereby opening doors of curiosity. What do you believe about cursing? Parents are cursing each other out in front of their children, thereby teaching children indirectly, to use profane language to express yourself. What do you believe about Sunday worship? Many parents let their children choose if they want to go to church or stay at home. Sometimes they take them to church, but do not require them to sit in service. Therefore they are not present in a worship experience. What do you believe about reading your bible? Parents, we have to have our own resolve before we can pass our faith down to our children.

We live during a time when so many people no longer have God consciousness. I was pondering some things about parenting and began to look at parenting and wonder why so many Christians are not passing our faith down to our children. I believe the Lord gave me a revelation. Many Christian parents are not growing in their own faith. Many are not maturing in their faith walk, so they are uncomfortable commanding their children after God. You can't give what you do not have to give. Parenting confidently in areas you are not challenging yourself to grow in is really impossible. Many are promoting carnal things to their children unaware. Growing as a parent should be intentional. Our senses have to be trained to discern confidently, causing us to parent boldly with little to no reluctancy.

It has always been God's desire for household blessings. Parents are to live in a way that we are always preparing for the next generation, not as the western culture's motto: me, myself and I. In this time that we live in, statistics show there are now more orphan children on the earth than at any other time in our history. There is a breakdown of the family structure which interrupts the passing down of household blessings.

If we are going to impact the future of this world we need to think generationally. Our children don't have to make the same mistakes we made. Our children don't have to dibble and dabble in drugs, premarital sex or have children out of wedlock. Our children don't have to go to prison to learn a lesson. What if we took more time to discern that child when he is three, four or five instead of thirteen, fourteen or fifteen?

Think about what would happen if parents didn't assume anything but began to discern what is going on with their children...find out who their children's friends are, observe more phone conversations, etc. How would that have affected your life and your children? What could you have been spared early in life had someone taken the time to discern?

What if you had listened to that inner voice when it said, "Something told me…"? What if your parents would have listened when they sensed, "He or she is not a good person for my child to be around?" God has equipped the world with a soul that connects us to God. It is through this eternal connection that we come to Christ. That is the part that will go back to God because all souls belong to God.

> "Behold, all souls are mine; as the soul of the
> father, so also the soul of the son is mine:"
> (Ezekiel 18:4a)

It is the part of us that yearns for God and His righteousness. When a child is withdrawn and normally he is people-oriented, ask why. When you do discern, don't assume you have all the answers.

When you validate something you sense, your response can't be reactionary because sometimes there is something more going on under the surface that you are missing. You may control the situation and miss the teaching opportunity that allows you to get to the heart of the matter.

Sometimes we are dealing with symptoms but have not dealt with the root problem. What would have happened if the parents of those children that walked into those high schools and slaughtered their classmates, had discerned the battles their children were encountering every day and what they were meditating on as a result of their pain?

Now I know parents that would say, "Go and sit down somewhere. You will be okay. That's normal. People treat people wrong all the time." However, you cannot assume how your child or anyone else's child is being affected by those situations. You have to discern your children. I realize that because there are more single-parent homes, more fatherless homes, motherless homes, and plain busy households, we need to find healthy outlets for our children. But nothing takes the place of that individual that God has placed in the child's life to aim the child in the way he should go. Each child has a unique path to follow. You know when your child is able to handle different situations, but only if you have spent the time to know.

So many families today think the bible does not recognize situations we face. Well, can you think about the seasons that you went through while you were growing up? What were some of the emotions you felt? What were some of the desires and struggles you had to deal with? Now flip the script. How are you responding to your child? Are you doing what was done to you and assuming that it is working or will work when it did not work for you? Or are you being overprotective because of the fear you have of history repeating itself? That's not discernment. That is insecurity. It is time to really get to know your child - not what you want to believe about your child, and not what you hope for your child - but how your child really is doing and relating to life. Lord, help us to seize each moment and opportunity to draw out of our children the thing that is lying beneath the surface in their hearts.

"Counsel in the heart of man is like deep water; but a man of understanding will draw it out."
(Proverbs 20:5)

Whatever you are passionate about you will indirectly promote in your home. Don't assume that just because you are passionate about church that you are teaching your children to be passionate about God. I am terribly afraid that many of us are passionate about religion or tradition and are passing down the church or denomination of mommy and daddy instead of the God of mommy or daddy. Many of us are passionate about education and we pass that passion to our children. Some are passionate about sports, crafts, arts, and music and we are passing that on to our children. Many have found God after trying so many other things and then finally someone introduces them to the God of the Bible and not a religion. Many of us attend church but have not manifested the kingdom of God in our families.

> "For the kingdom of God is not meat and drink, but righteousness, and peace, and joy in the Holy Ghost."
> (Romans 14:17)

IN CONCLUSION

You are all on assignment and should return to God's intention. He has given you this opportunity to return and repent for whatever the distraction has been and to begin to partner with the Lord again to see God's purposes unfold in the life of God's inheritance. Let's raise a godly generation that won't forget God because you have lovingly been there to Discern The Season Of Your Children.

Your ministry, your business and your personal development are all wonderful aspirations. They are nice commodities that can create nice cushions and great heirlooms to pass down as inheritance to your children, but they can all be burned in the fire or even disappear and be squandered away. I want you to always remember instead of only focusing on an inheritance for your family, stop and remember God has already given you an inheritance that will last eternally!

3   Children are ·a gift [an inheritance] from the Lord; ·babies [the fruit of the womb] are a reward.

4   Children ·who are born to a young man [of one's youth] are like arrows in the hand of a warrior [they help in the challenges and conflicts of life].

5   Happy [Blessed] is the man who has his ·bag [quiver] full of ·arrows [them]. They will not be ·defeated [humiliated] when they ·fight [L speak to] their enemies at the city gate [the central place of commerce and government].

(Psalms 127:3-5)

RITES OF PASSAGE

The Bible Says This:

> "While the earth remains, seedtime and harvest,
> cold and heat, winter and summer, and day and
> night shall not cease."
> (Genesis 8:22)

> "6 Go to the ant, thou sluggard; consider her ways,
> and be wise: 7 Which having no guide, overseer,
> or ruler, 8 provideth her meat in the summer, and
> gathereth her food in the harvest."
> (Proverbs 6:6-8)

> "The ants are not a strong people, but they prepare
> their food in the summer…"
> (Proverbs 30:25)

Each season is a significant time in your life as you develop into who God has called you to be. Never think you have no hope because you have entered into a different season. Just find out what kind of preparation you have to do or what kind of maintenance is needed at this time. God equips you as you enter a new season with fresh insight and anticipation of God's perspective and provision.

As I look at our global society the Catholics have a confirmation, African tribes have rites of passage and the Jewish family has a bar mitzvah. All represent a rites of passage. It amazes me that the Christian family has been engrafted in as spiritual Jews, but we have not embraced the teaching that God commanded the Jewish family to adhere too.

Rites of Passage MSN Encarta Online (2001).

"Rites of Passage, ceremonies that mark a person's progress from one role, phase of life, or social status to another. The term was first used by Belgian anthropologist, Arnold van Gennep. The basic life changes are birth, puberty, marriage, and death. Each change is marked by a transitional period involving specific rituals: removal of the individual from his or her former status; suspension from normal social contact; and readmission into society in the newly acquired status.

This transitional process sometimes provides others with the opportunity to adjust to the event, as… the death of a loved one. Rites of passage occur in all societies and often involve symbolism and reaffirm the values of a society".

Rites of Passage Ceremony

People often ask me to provide information on how I carry out our Rites of Passage. This is a subject dear to my heart. It has been incorporated in our family since my first daughter graduated middle school. I would like to share the journey with you:

Sample Letter To Mentor

Growing up is something a lot of people fear. There is just something about leaving adolescence that puts people in a gripping state of anxiety. My family does not believe in being afraid of moving to the next stage of life. As an 8th grade graduate moving into high school, it can be very scary. At this time in life a child is discovering who she is, what she believes, who her true friends are, and how she perceives herself. A healthy transition to "womanhood" is a necessity for a young girl figuring out who she is. Having three sisters, two of whom are older than me and one younger, my parents decided to create a ceremony celebrating this milestone. The "Rites of Passage," as we like to call it, is a ceremony in our girls' lives that is held to establish who they uniquely are and the commitments they have to their faith.

To begin the process of the Rites of Passage, I select several spiritually strong women who are usually family members or close family friends who each have an ample amount of wisdom to pass down to an inquisitive young girl. Then my daughter will meet with them at a meal, one at a time, to learn and soak in all of their knowledge (Time is approximately one to two hours).

A DAUGHTER'S RITES OF PASSAGE STORY

The first woman who imparted into my life was my Aunt. My Aunt taught me "what makes me beautiful." She told me that whatever God has equipped me with, my gifts, talents, and personality, will help me be the best that I can be. She taught me that I maintain my beauty by staying in communication with God. Overall, she taught me to remember how very important it is to be God's perspective of beauty because that is what makes me a living, walking, loving witness of His beauty. The following day, my mother's friend poured into my life. She taught me how to be a good communicator. She taught me that I should always communicate with humility. She conveyed to me the importance of knowing the value of silence. The next day, another one of my mother's friends spoke with me. She assured me that being different is okay. She told me that I should know who I am in Christ and not who I am according to what others believe I should be. She gave me an important scripture that remains with me even to this day. The scripture states, "Do not conform any longer to the patterns of this world, but be transformed by the renewing of your mind (Romans 12:2)." She informed me to not copy the behavior and customs of this world, and to let God transform me by the way I think. At the end of this three-day journey into finding who I am, I put together a speech that I was to present for all of my family and friends to hear. I came to a point in my life where I knew who I was. I knew that I was beautiful and that God's perception of me is what mattered most. I knew how to communicate effectively. And most importantly, I left with the belief that I don't have to conform to what everyone else is doing. I was able to share this with the people I love. At the end of my Rites of passage, my father presented me with a purity ring that symbolizes me becoming a woman and represented my commitment in purity until I have a husband. This is something instilled in my heart and I will stand for these values for as long as I am here on this earth. Today, I am able to confidently strive for everything I want in life. As an eighth-grade graduate moving to High school, I would have never guessed that those values instilled in me then, would remain with me today.

Sample Topic and Format

A WOMAN AND HER MINISTRY

(Assigned To: NAME)

Goal of Conversation: As a woman who has been an important "minister" in DAUGHTER'S NAME' life YOU will charge DAUGHTER'S NAME to fulfill her part in the larger body of Christ.

Possible Bible Passages: • I Corinthians 12:27 (We are an important part of the body) • I Timothy 4:12 (Even the young should minister) • 2 Corinthians 5:18 (All are called to the ministry of reconciliation)

Suggestions:

- Tell about when/how you knew you were called to minister
- Tell why "ministry" isn't just limited to those in vocational church ministry
- Talk about the need to remain connected to the church and to eventually guide a family by taking them to church and serving, etc.

- Emphasize the overall "ministry of reconciliation" to which all of us are called
- Possibly touch upon how you've seen DAUGHTER'S NAME serve and possible places/ situations in which she may be called to "minister" in the future such as in college, the workplace, at church, at home, in the community, etc.

The Charge: End the letter with a "charge" to DAUGHTER'S NAME to take responsibility to always seek a place to use her gifts in God's service. Possible Gift/Symbol: A toy hand/ear/foot – signifying that DAUGHTER'S NAME is part of the larger body of Christ

Sample Letter From Our Pastor

Dear DAUGHTER'S NAME,

CONGRATULATIONS!

You've reached an important time in your life, not only because you graduated with honors, but because you are now moving into your high school career, which really does mark a rite of passage.

In the months and years ahead, you will be given many more privileges and opportunities to make your own decisions. Your parents will continue to guide you, but they will trust you more and more to make right choices for your future.

I know that they have provided you a great foundation, and your own walk with the Lord and understanding of His Word also gives you the principles you will need to excel in school and succeed in life.

XXXX and I pray God's best blessings for you, and that His favor will surround you like a shield (Psalm 5:12) from this day forward!

XXX XXXX
Senior Pastor

Sample Letter of Request To Family

I am having a ceremony on (date) to bless (Child Name). This is a tradition we do every time one of our children enters high school. We call this ceremony a Rites of Passage. It is a lot like a Jewish Bat Mitzvah, a celebration of a significant milestone in their life. When many young people enter their teens and high school these years are called the wandering years by society. Many do not know who they are or where they are going in life...so my husband and I intentionally point our daughters toward the target that God has set for our Christian family. During this time, we tell them who they are and the legacy they have inherited, and my husband gives my daughter a promise ring. This ring represents a vow they make to God and to their father to maintain their purity until marriage.

I want to include the (our family). We would love for you to share a wisdom thought and/or blessing because our family has a great legacy.

Please email me your letters by (Date) if you are willing to participate. It would mean a lot to have the aunts and uncles represented.

Love you much,

Terrilyn

Sample Letter from A Great Aunt

You are a beautiful, exceptional, and unique individual who is wonderfully and beautifully made in the image of the Lord. This fact is not limited to when you are born, become a toddler, entered into kindergarten, then to elementary school, to middle school, or high school, then to college, then off into a life of adulthood, marriage, children, grandchildren then to being retired and empty nesting. No, this wonderfully made DAUGHTER'S NAME is wonderfully made each and every day of her life until her death. Along the path of this wonderfully made young woman's life, though, there will be detours, areas where the bridge might be out, major decisions that will be life changing, and issues that only the Lord can resolve. There will also be challenges, lifestyle adjustments, valleys of decisions, crossroads that must be diligently and carefully decided upon, peer pressures from individuals who think they know what's better for your life than God himself, not to mention emotional cares and concerns within you as a result of all of these concerns.

Consequently, it is going to be up to this wonderful, awesome, powerful, and all knowing God of yours who wonderfully made you to bring you to it, keep you while you are in it, and bring you out of it successfully, victoriously, and to his glory and his alone. The "It" we are talking about is whatever cares, concerns, trials, and traps of the enemy of your soul that life dishes out to you. Never run from Satan, but stand still to see the salvation of the Lord in every situation life dishes out to you. Just know that life has no sorrow that heaven cannot heal. It starts with this transition you now face from junior high to high school. Always remember, DAUGHTER'S NAME, that you are the only one of your kind because there is no carbon copy of you anywhere. There is no river wide enough, no mountain tall enough, and not valley deep enough that DAUGHTER'S NAME can not master, get through, and endure with the direct help of the Lord your God, It is now time for you to exercise all the values your parents, grandparents, aunties, uncles, church family, and the Lord has instilled in you from the very first breath you took until this very moment in your life. Don't allow any human being to take you off of that path, DAUGH-TER'S NAME. Use the very identity the Lord has given you up until this time to carry you to this new level you are now facing, to carry you through it, and out of it as you proceed down the divine path God has chosen for your life. Don't allow anyone to control the "you" they did not create and cannot force to do anything against your will. Take the Lord along with you into this next phase, DAUGH-TER'S NAME, and I can assure you, you will make it to it, through it, and out of it successfully with the help of the God of your salvation, but, remember to keep the Lord first, your family second (or your husband after you get married) and then everyone else. May God's richest blessings be yours, always, in Jesus' awesome name.

I Love you,

Aunt XXXXX

Acknowledgments

Giving ALL the glory to God for grace, grace, grace and more grace to steward what you have placed in my hands. This book was birthed out of obedience to your voice; the editor and publishing consultant were selected by the Holy Spirit. I could not have done this without YOU! Lord I release this book into your hands for you to do what you will.

Thank you, November Media Publishing, for trusting me as your first consultant client. Your grace, wisdom and knowledge gave me the strategic process to complete this assignment!

Thank you, Destined To Publish, for being a part of my writing journey. Thank you for providing a place for scribes to gather to receive resources and guidance on their writing journey.

Thank you to my cousin and content editor, Sylvia Vines. You edited my first book, Discerning the Season of Your Children, and this one. Thank you for your excellence and attention to detail.

Thank you to my honey, Alan, for 30+ years of marriage. Thank you for unconditional love and being the best example of the Father's love to our daughters. Thank you Alaynia, Alynn, Alyssa, and Alexis for choosing the God of your parents over and over again, even when it meant walking alone. It is an honor to call you all my daughters.

Thank you to my sister, Crystal, a constant reminder of grandma's hospitality to her neices. And to all of my siblings and family in love, framily (Friends/Family), and prayer partners, I love you! Thank you for loving and praying. Thank you to my closest friends that love me at all times. You know who you are.

Connect with Terrilyn Franklin

Website: www.arrowsinmyhand.com
Email: TerrilynFranklin2@gmail.com